BRIGHT IDEA BOOKS

VETERINARIAN

by Marne Ventura

CAPSTONE PRESS
a capstone imprint

Bright Idea Books are published by Capstone Press
1710 Roe Crest Drive, North Mankato, Minnesota 56003
www.mycapstone.com

Library of Congress Cataloging-in-Publication Data
Names: Ventura, Marne, author.
Title: Veterinarian / by Marne Ventura.
Description: North Mankato, Minnesota : Bright Idea Books, an imprint of
    Capstone Press, [2019] | Series: Jobs with animals | Audience: Age 9-12. |
    Audience: Grade 4 to 6. | Includes bibliographical references and index.
Identifiers: LCCN 2018035990 | ISBN 9781543557817 (hardcover : alk. paper) |
    ISBN 9781543558135 (ebook) | ISBN 9781543560435 (paperback)
Subjects: LCSH: Veterinarians--Vocational guidance--Juvenile literature.
Classification: LCC SF756.28 .V46 2019 | DDC 636.089/069--dc23
LC record available at https://lccn.loc.gov/2018035990

Editorial Credits
Editor: Meg Gaertner
Designer: Becky Daum
Production Specialist: Dan Peluso

Photo Credits
iStockphoto: andresr, 17, BartCo, 26–27, BraunS, 30–31, kali9, 5, 10–11, 18–19, 28,
Mypurgatoryyears, 14–15, ptaxa, 12–13, SashaFoxWalters, 25, SelectStock, cover, zilli, 13
Shutterstock Images: belizar, 6–7, ChameleonsEye, 9, David Tadevosian, 22–23, Deborah Kolb, 21

Printed in the United States of America.
PA48

TABLE OF CONTENTS

CHAPTER 1

VETERINARIAN

Animals are important to people in many ways. Pets are friends. Service dogs help people. Farmers raise animals for food. Sometimes animals get hurt or sick. They are taken to a veterinarian. A vet is an animal doctor.

4

Vets **treat** sick animals. They care for hurt animals. They give animals **vaccines**. They operate when an animal needs surgery.

Vets give regular checkups to make sure animals are healthy.

Vets work with all kinds of animals. People bring pets to a vet **clinic**. Vets visit animals in zoos. They help the wild animals. Vets go to farms. They make sure animals raised for food stay healthy. Vets also treat animals used in sports. These include racehorses and racing dogs.

Do you like taking care of animals? Maybe a job as a veterinarian is for you.

Vets care for a maned wolf puppy at a zoo.

CHAPTER 2

QUALITIES AND Skills

Good veterinarians have many personal qualities. Vets like working with many kinds of animals. They care for cats and dogs. They also help birds, lizards, and snakes. Some might treat cows or horses. Others help zoo animals such as tigers or giraffes.

A zoo vet handles an injured koala.

Veterinarians have a big job. Owners trust them with their animals' health. Vets are caring. They feel comfortable around animals. Vets need to work well with people too. Vets tell owners how to care for their animals. They explain what is wrong when an animal is sick or hurt. They help owners as well as animals.

Good vets work well with both people and animals.

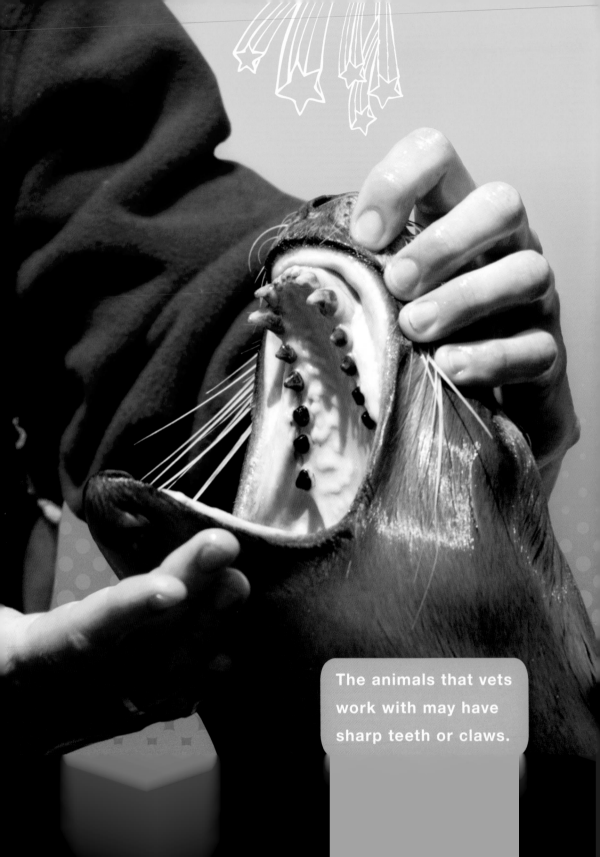

The animals that vets work with may have sharp teeth or claws.

Some baby animals drink milk from a bottle.

Working with animals can be hard. A puppy might not hold still. A bird might bite. A cat might scratch. Lions and tigers can hurt people. Vets need to be brave and strong. They also need to be careful.

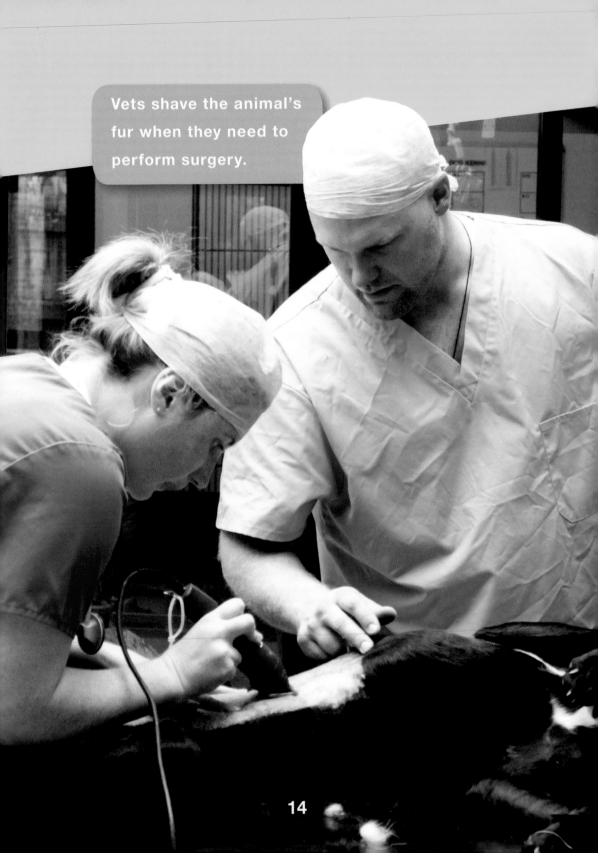

Vets shave the animal's fur when they need to perform surgery.

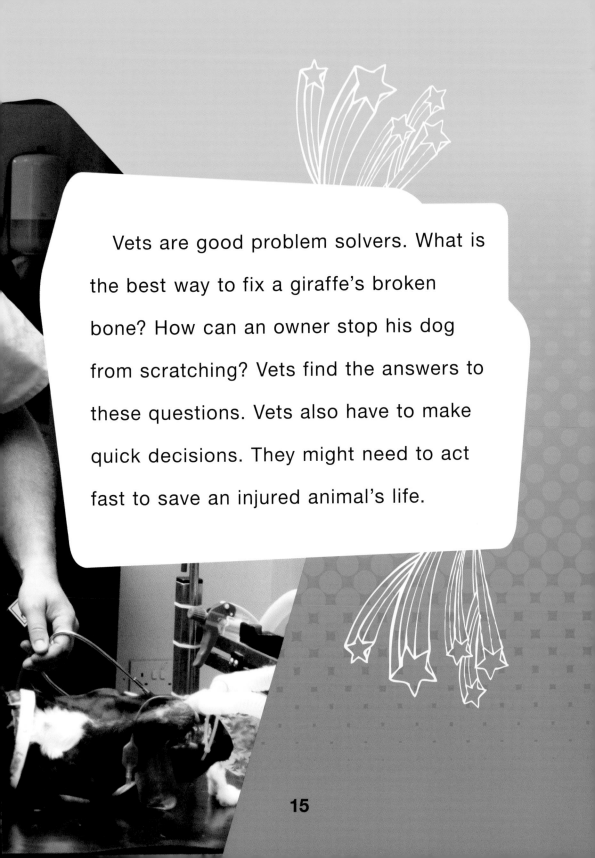

Vets are good problem solvers. What is the best way to fix a giraffe's broken bone? How can an owner stop his dog from scratching? Vets find the answers to these questions. Vets also have to make quick decisions. They might need to act fast to save an injured animal's life.

CHAPTER 3

SCHOOL FOR Vets

Vets go to college for eight years. First they get a four-year **degree**. People can get degrees in **animal science** or **zoology**. Then they go through a vet program. Not every college has this program.

There are 28 vet schools in the United States. Students might need to travel to a different state for vet school.

Vet students learn about the body parts of different animals.

Would you like to be a vet? You can start learning now. Get good grades in school. Take lots of math and science classes. Read books about animals. Watch TV shows about animals. Visit the zoo.

COLLEGE PROGRAMS

Some colleges have two-year programs for jobs with animals. These prepare students to be vet technicians, nurses, and assistants.

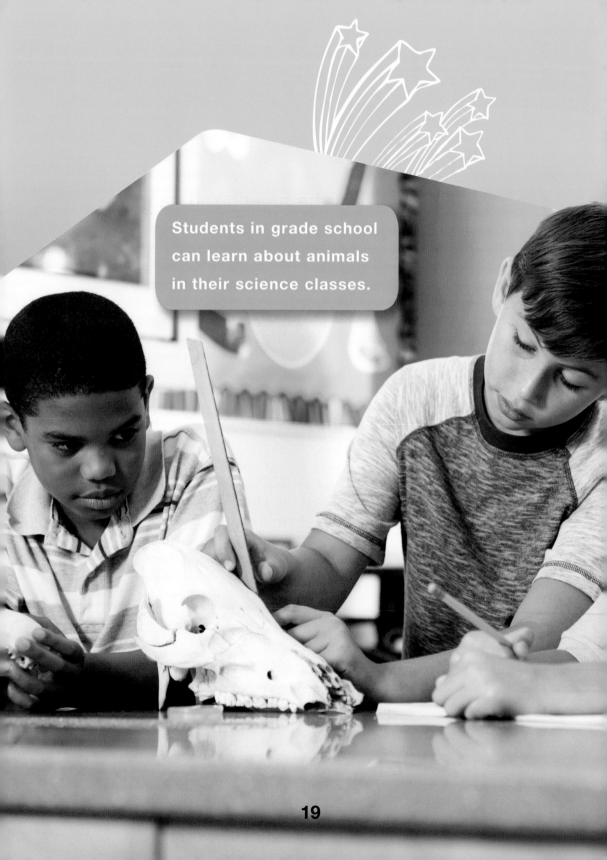

Students in grade school can learn about animals in their science classes.

CHAPTER 4

GETTING
Experience

It takes a lot of practice to be a vet. Any work with animals helps. There are many ways to get this experience. Some families have pets. Taking care of a pet is good experience for a future vet.

Maybe a friend or neighbor needs help. Take a friend's dog for a walk. Play with and feed the neighbors' cat while they are away.

Dog walking is an easy way to get experience with animals.

Some pet shelters need **volunteers**. These volunteers help feed the animals. They clean animals' homes. They give the animals attention. They play with the animals. Some zoos and wild animal parks have volunteer programs too.

4-H

People can also join organizations such as 4-H. 4-H is a U.S. organization. It helps kids learn about health, science, farming, citizenship, and more. 4-H members often raise animals.

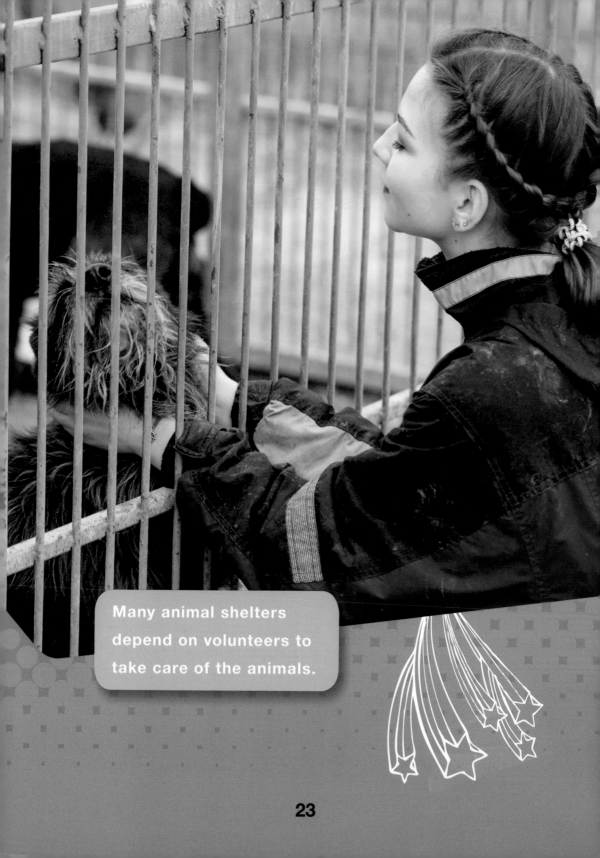

Many animal shelters depend on volunteers to take care of the animals.

CHAPTER 5

WHERE Vets Work

Vets work in many places. Most vets work in clinics. They help pets such as dogs, cats, and birds.

Other vets go to animals' homes. They might go to a dairy farm to help cows. They might visit a zoo to care for a sick bear. They might go to a racetrack to check on a horse.

Vets can focus on equine practice, which is the care of horses.

Some vets work in **laboratories**. They do research. They study ways to better care for animals. Other vets work in schools. They are teachers. They teach animal science. They help others become vets.

A vet teaches students about how to care for sheep.

UNDER OATH

When students become vets, they make a promise. It is called the Veterinarian's **Oath**. Vets promise to help animals.

It is a good time for people who want to be vets. Vet jobs pay well. Vets earn around $88,000 per year on average. The number of vet jobs is also growing.

GLOSSARY

animal science
the study of animals that are under the control of humans

clinic
a place to get medical care

degree
an academic award given to students after they complete a course of study

laboratory
a place where scientists do research

oath
a promise

treat
to give medical care to

vaccine
medicine given to prevent illness

volunteer
someone who works without pay

zoology
the study of the behavior and physical traits of animals

OTHER JOBS TO CONSIDER

VETERINARY ASSISTANT

Assistants help keep the clinic clean and organized. They help care for the animals. They also give information to pet owners.

VETERINARY NURSE

Nurses take care of the animals at clinics. They teach pet owners about animal health.

VETERINARY TECHNICIAN

Technicians help veterinarians by giving medical tests. They prepare animals for operations.

ACTIVITY

BECOMING A VET

Not sure if a career as a veterinarian is for you? Here are some activities to help you decide. First, read books from your library about being a vet. Then make two lists. The first is a list of what you would like about being a vet. The second is a list about what you might not like.

Consider talking to a vet about the job. See if you can schedule a time to meet with the vet. Make a list of questions ahead of time. If you have a pet, you can also go along on a vet visit. You can see what the vet is like in action. Watch as he or she takes care of your pet. What qualities does he or she have?

FURTHER RESOURCES

Curious about vets? Learn more here:

Science Buddies: Veterinarian
www.sciencebuddies.org/science-engineering-careers/life-sciences/
    veterinarian

Trueit, Trudi Strain. *Veterinarian*. New York: Cavendish Square, 2014.

Interested in other jobs with animals? Check out these resources:

Bedell, J. M. So, *You Want to Work with Animals? Discover Fantastic Ways to Work with Animals, from Veterinary Science to Aquatic Biology*. New York: Aladdin, 2017.

PBS Learning Media: Zoo Veterinarian
https://tpt.pbslearningmedia.org/resource/c193b6cc-c520-4ac8-aea6-
    0b624fe83fa8/zoo-veterinarian/

Shaw, Gina. *Curious about Zoo Vets*. New York: Penguin, 2015.

INDEX

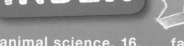